I0457307

GRANDMA MARGIE'S TALE OF THE ABC'S OF THE BIBLE

Written by Dr. K.T. Zulkowski

Copyright © 2023 by Dr. K.T. Zulkowski

All rights reserved. No part of this book may be reproduced or transmitted in any form or by anymeans, electronic or mechanical, including photocopying, recording, or by any information storage and retrieval system, without permission in writing from the publisher.

Published by Mz. Kim Productions

4263 Tierra Rejada Rd #151

Moorpark, CA 93021

www.mzkimproductions.com

ISBN: 978-1-962106-16-0

Printed in United States of America

First Printing: August 2023

Date of Copyright: July 5,2023

For permissions, please contact: Mz. Kim Productions

4263 Tierra Rejada Rd #151

Moorpark, CA 93021

www.mzkimproductions.com

mzkimproductions@gmail.com

The characters and events portrayed in this book are fictitious. Any similarity to real persons, living or dead, is purely coincidental and not intended by the author.

Dedication

To all the children who are curious and eager to learn, May this book ignite your imagination and deepen your faith. May you find joy in the stories and teachings of the Bible, And may it be a guiding light throughout your journey. To the parents and grandparents who instill love and values, Thank you for nurturing the hearts and minds of the young. May this book be a tool for shared moments and cherished memories, As you pass down the wisdom of the ages from generation to generation. To the Sunday school teachers who inspire and educate, Thank you for your tireless dedication and unwavering passion. May this book be a valuable resource in your teaching, As you shape the lives of children and guide them towards a life of faith. And to Grandma Margie, the wise and loving grandmother, Whose spirit and teachings inspired this book. May your legacy of love and wisdom continue to touch lives, And may your stories forever live on in the hearts of children. This book is dedicated to all those who seek knowledge and embrace the power of storytelling. May it be a source of inspiration and enlightenment, and may its impact be felt for generations to come.

With heartfelt gratitude,

Dr. K.T. Zulkowski

Educational Value

"Grandma Margie's ABC's of the Bible" is an invaluable educational resource for children, parents, and educators alike. It introduces young readers to the foundational stories and teachings of the Bible in a fun and engaging way. By learning the ABC's, children not only develop their language and literacy skills but also gain a solid understanding of important biblical concepts and values.

The book fosters a love for reading and encourages children to explore the Bible further. Each page is filled with colorful illustrations that bring the stories to life, making it easier for children to connect with and remember the lessons. The interactive approach, including activities and quizzes, reinforces the learning and allows children to actively participate in the educational process.

Through the stories of Adam and Eve, Moses, Jesus, and many others, children learn about faith, love, forgiveness, and the importance of living a life that pleases God. The book instills important values such as kindness, compassion, and obedience, helping children develop a strong moral compass.

"Grandma Margie's ABC's of the Bible" is not only educational but also promotes a deeper understanding of God's love and His teachings. It lays a strong foundation of faith that can accompany children throughout their lives, guiding them in making wise choices and nurturing their spiritual growth.

Overall, this book is an excellent tool for introducing young minds to the wonders of the Bible, fostering a love for learning, and nurturing their spiritual development.

Grandma Margie: Welcome, my dear Zipporah and Zion!

Today, we will learn the **ABC's** of the Bible. Are you ready?

Zipporah and Zion: Yes, Grandma Margie!

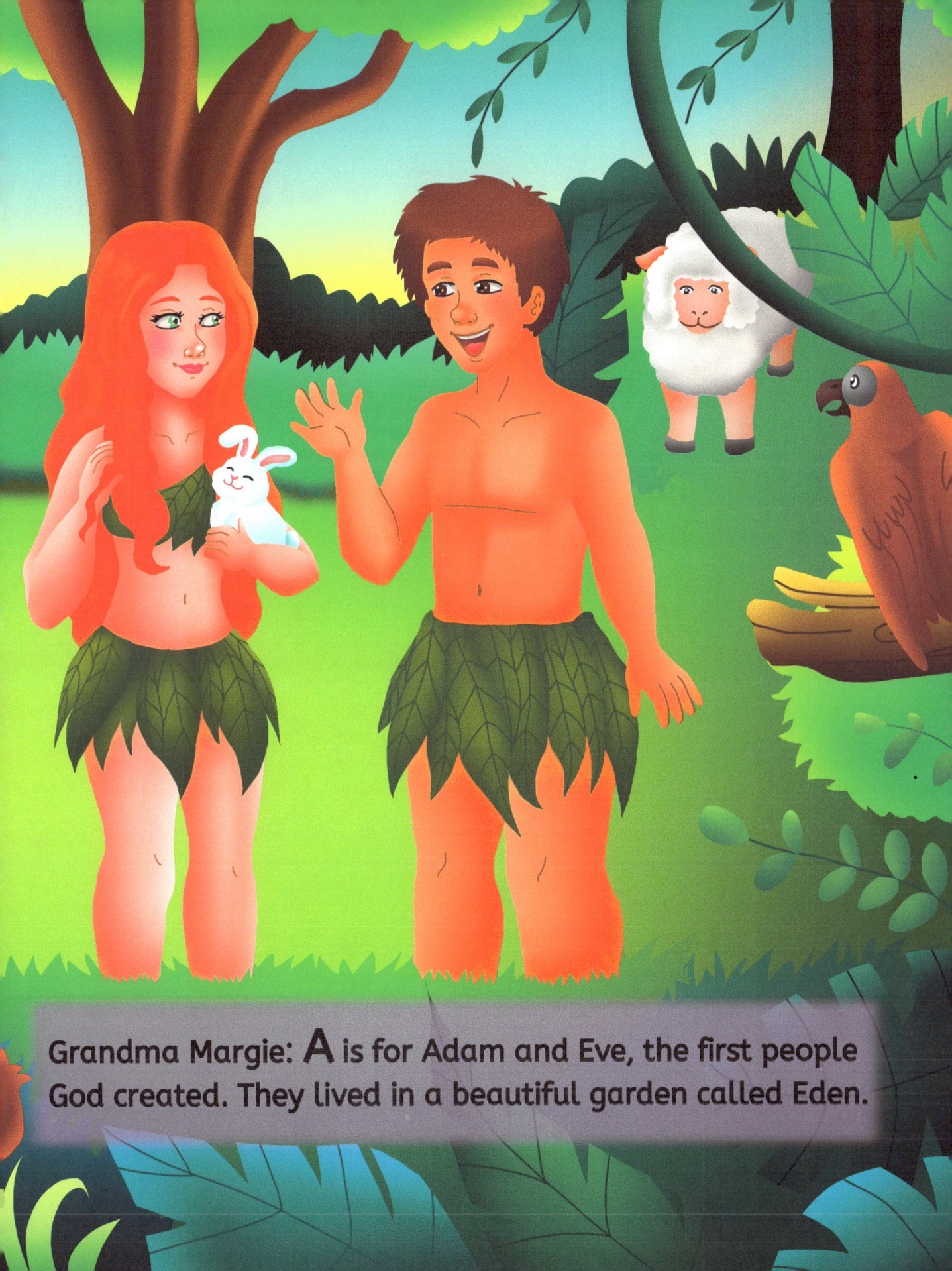

Grandma Margie: **A** is for Adam and Eve, the first people God created. They lived in a beautiful garden called Eden.

Zion: Grandma, what's the Burning Bush?

Grandma Margie: B is for the Burning Bush, where God spoke to Moses and called him to lead His people out of Egypt.

Zipporah: Grandma, what are the Ten Commandments?

Grandma Margie: C is for the Ten Commandments, the rules God gave to His people to live by. They teach us how to love God and others.

Zion: Grandma, who is David?

Grandma Margie: D is for David, a young shepherd boy who defeated the giant Goliath with God's help. It shows us that with faith, we can overcome any challenge.

Zipporah: Grandma, why is the tomb empty?

Grandma Margie: **E** is for the Empty Tomb, where Jesus rose from the dead. It reminds us of God's power and love for us.

Zion: Grandma, what are the Fruits of the Spirit?

Grandma Margie: **F** is for the Fruits of the Spirit, which are love, joy, peace, patience, kindness, goodness, faithfulness, gentleness, and self-control. They help us grow closer to God and others.

Zipporah: Grandma, who is the Good Samaritan?

Grandma Margie: G is for the Good Samaritan, a kind person who helped someone in need. It teaches us to love and care for others, no matter who they are.

Zion: Grandma, what is the Holy Spirit?

Grandma Margie: H is for the Holy Spirit, who is God's presence with us. The Holy Spirit guides and helps us in our daily lives.

Zipporah: Grandma, who are Isaac and Abraham?

Grandma Margie: I is for Isaac and Abraham. Abraham was a faithful man who trusted God, and Isaac was his son. They teach us about faith and obedience.

Zion: Grandma, who is Jesus?

Grandma Margie: J is for Jesus, God's Son, who came to earth to save us. He showed us how to love and live a life pleasing to God.

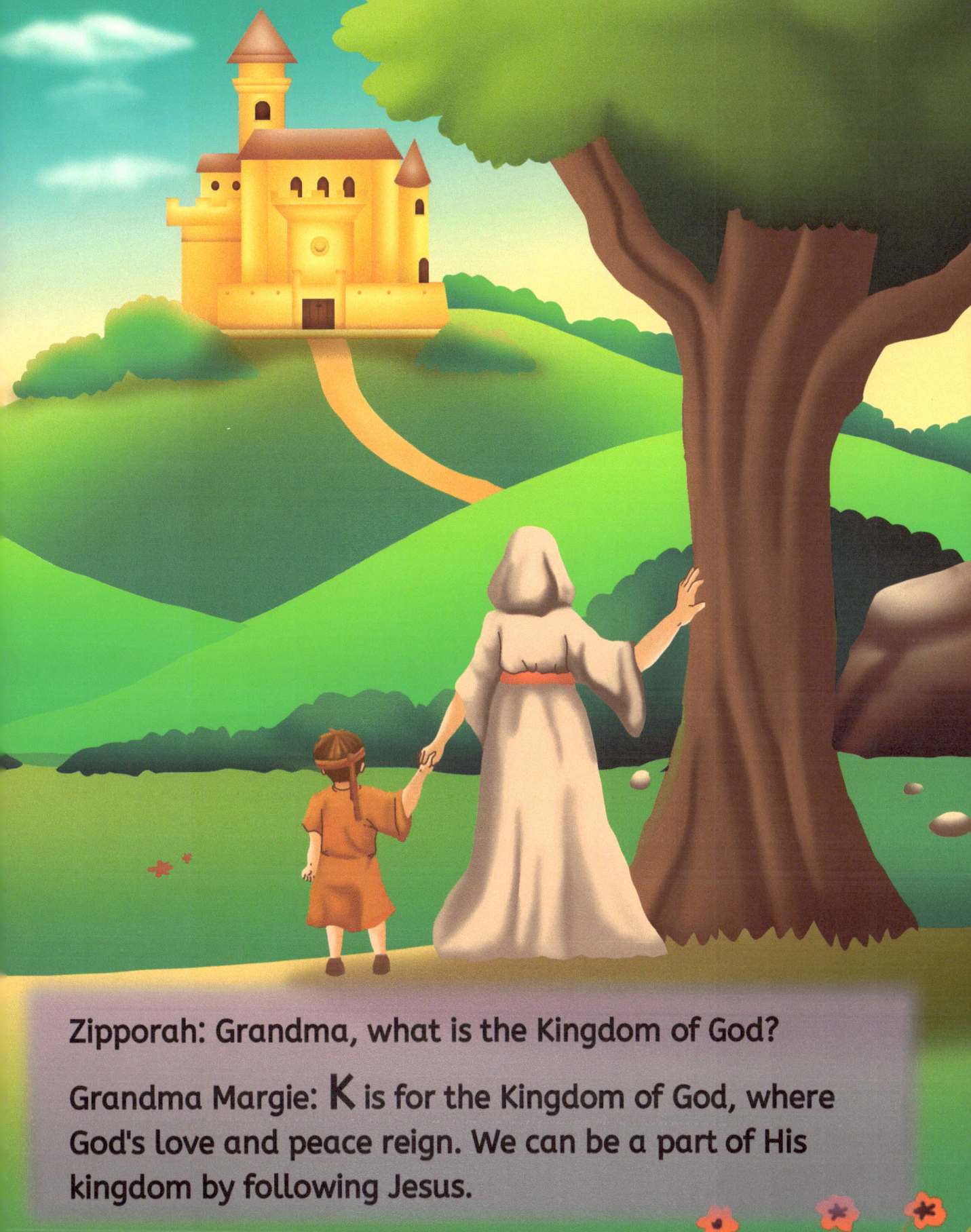

Zipporah: Grandma, what is the Kingdom of God?

Grandma Margie: K is for the Kingdom of God, where God's love and peace reign. We can be a part of His kingdom by following Jesus.

"Our Father, who art in heaven,
Hallowed be thy name.
Thy Kingdom come.
Thy will be done on earth as it is in heaven.
Give us this day our daily bread.
And forgive us our trespasses, as we forgive those who trespass against us.
And lead us not into temptation,
But deliver us from evil.
For thine is the kingdom, the power and the glory for ever and ever.
Amen"

Zion: Grandma, what is the Lord's Prayer?

Grandma Margie: L is for the Lord's Prayer, a special prayer Jesus taught us. It helps us communicate with God and ask for His guidance and provision.

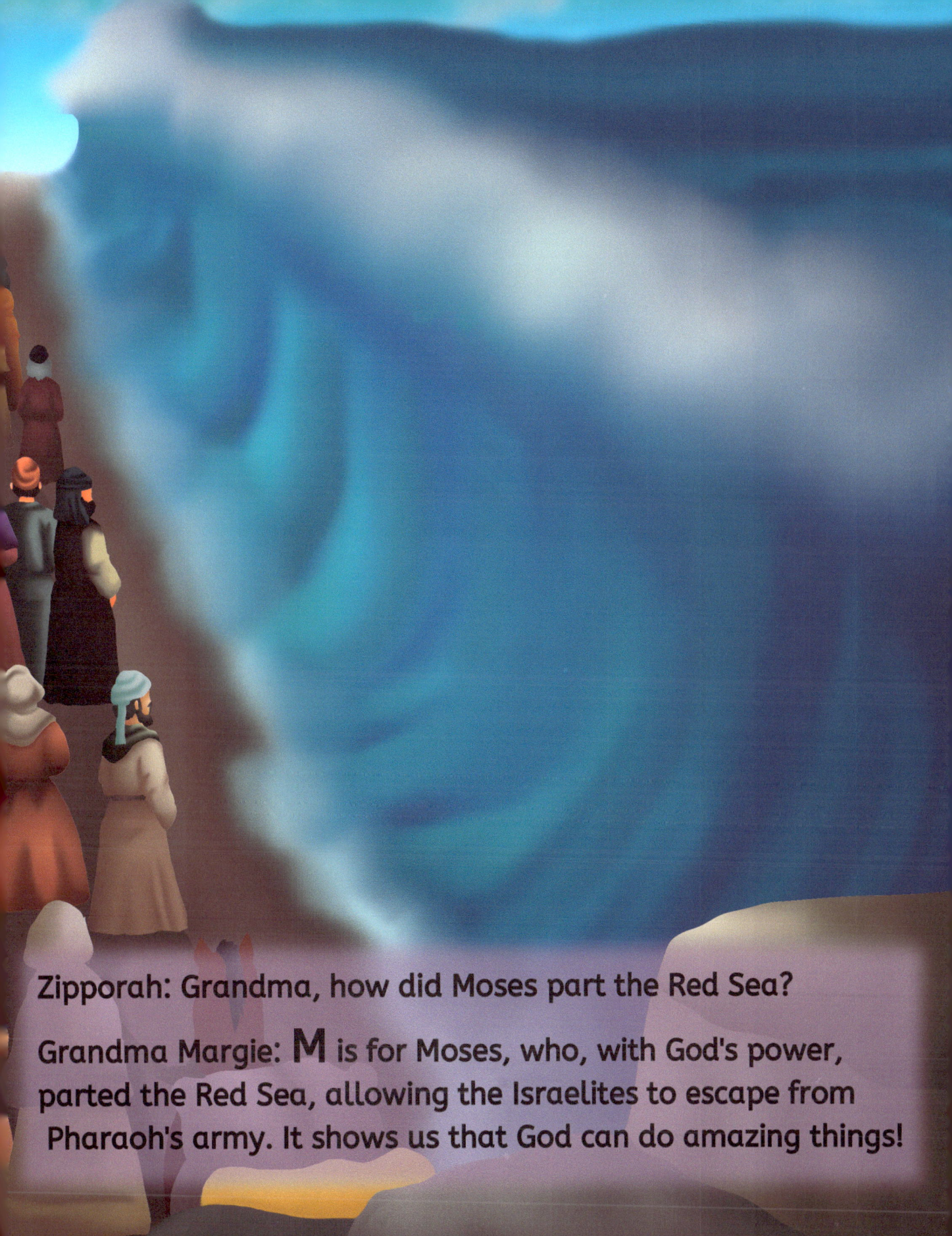

Zipporah: Grandma, how did Moses part the Red Sea?

Grandma Margie: M is for Moses, who, with God's power, parted the Red Sea, allowing the Israelites to escape from Pharaoh's army. It shows us that God can do amazing things!

Zion: Grandma, why did Noah build an ark?

Grandma Margie: N is for Noah's Ark. God asked Noah to build it to save him, his family, and the animals from a great flood. It reminds us of God's faithfulness and protection.

Zipporah: Grandma, why is the olive branch important?

Grandma Margie: O is for the Olive Branch, a symbol of peace. After the flood, Noah sent out a dove, and it returned with an olive branch, showing that the land was safe again.

Zion: Grandma, who is the Prodigal Son?

Grandma Margie: P is for the Prodigal Son, a story Jesus told about a son who left his father but returned, and his father forgave him. It teaches us about God's unconditional love and forgiveness.

Zipporah: Grandma, who is the Queen of Sheba?

Grandma Margie: Q is for the Queen of Sheba, a wise and wealthy queen who visited King Solomon. It reminds us that God blesses us with wisdom and riches when we seek Him.

Zion: Grandma, what is the Resurrection?

Grandma Margie: R is for the Resurrection, when Jesus rose from the dead. It is the most important event in the Bible, showing us that Jesus conquered death and gives us eternal life.

Zipporah: Grandma, what is the Sermon on the Mount?

Grandma Margie: S is for the Sermon on the Mount, where Jesus taught His disciples and the crowd about love, forgiveness, and living a life that pleases God.

Zion: Grandma, what happened at the Tower of Babel?

Grandma Margie: T is for the Tower of Babel, where people tried to build a tower to reach heaven. But God confused their languages, teaching us the importance of humility and unity.

Zipporah: Grandma, what is unconditional love?

Grandma Margie: U is for the Unconditional Love of God. God loves us no matter what, and His love is never-ending and without conditions. It's the greatest love we can zever experience.

Zion: Grandma, what does the vine and branches mean?

Grandma Margie: V is for the Vine and Branches. Jesus said, "I am the vine, and you are the branches." It teaches us that when we stay connected to Jesus, we bear good fruit and grow in our faith.

Zipporah: Grandma, who were the Wise Men?

Grandma Margie: W is for the Wise Men, who followed a star to find baby Jesus and brought Him gifts. They teach us about seeking and worshiping Jesus with all our hearts.

Zion: Grandma, what does example mean?

Grandma Margie: X is for eXample. Jesus is our perfect example of how to live a life pleasing to God. We can learn from His teachings and actions.

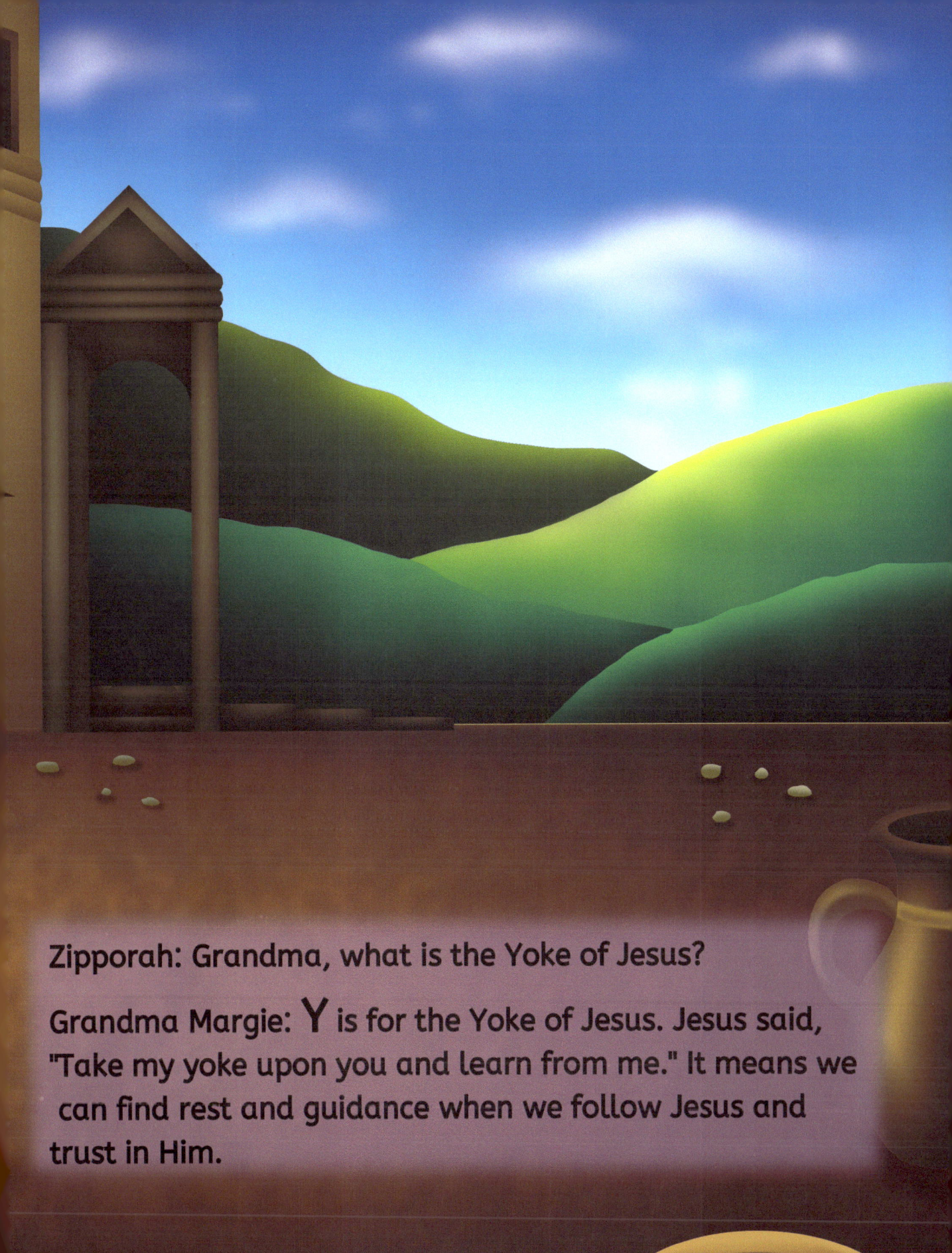

Zipporah: Grandma, what is the Yoke of Jesus?

Grandma Margie: Y is for the Yoke of Jesus. Jesus said, "Take my yoke upon you and learn from me." It means we can find rest and guidance when we follow Jesus and trust in Him.

Zion: Grandma, who is Zacchaeus?

Grandma Margie: Z is for Zacchaeus, a tax collector who climbed a tree to see Jesus. Jesus noticed him and changed his life. It shows us that Jesus loves and forgives everyone, no matter their past.

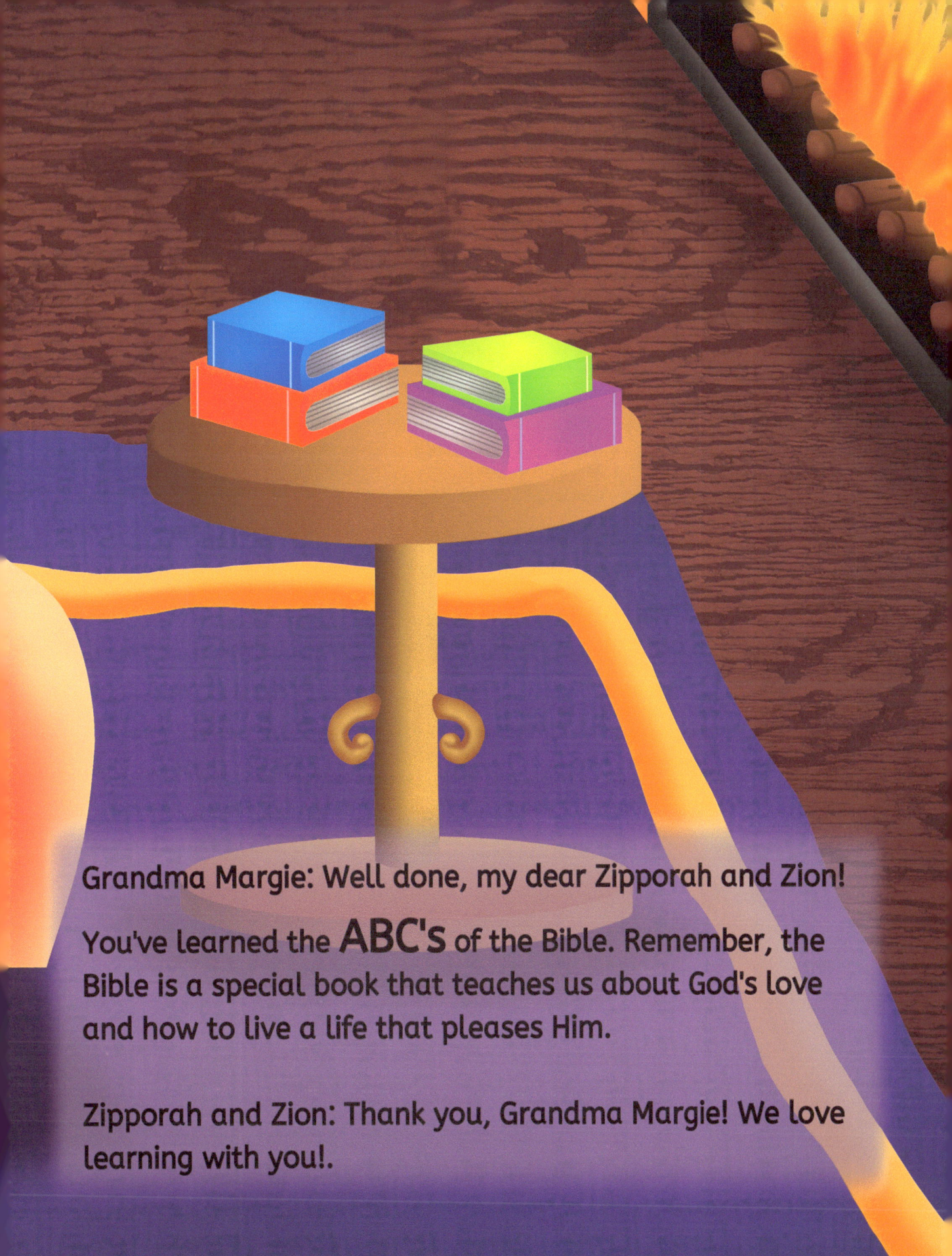

Grandma Margie: Well done, my dear Zipporah and Zion!

You've learned the ABC's of the Bible. Remember, the Bible is a special book that teaches us about God's love and how to live a life that pleases Him.

Zipporah and Zion: Thank you, Grandma Margie! We love learning with you!.

Author's Note

Author's Note: Dear Reader,

Thank you for joining us on this incredible journey of faith, love, and learning with Grandma Margie's ABC's of the Bible. It is truly a joy to be able to share this heartwarming and educational children's book with you. As a renowned author and award-winning filmmaker, I have always believed in the power of storytelling to connect and inspire. With this book, my focus is to introduce children to the foundational stories and teachings of the Bible in a fun and engaging way. Through the wisdom and love of Grandma Margie, young readers will embark on a fun adventure of learning and discovery. Each letter of the alphabet represents a significant aspect of the Bible, allowing children to explore timeless biblical concepts in a meaningful and memorable manner. From the resurrection of Christ to the Good Samaritan, and from the Sermon on the Mount to stories of faith, courage, and love, this book covers it all. The captivating storytelling and beautiful illustrations will capture the imagination of young readers, fostering a love for the Word of God. But this book is not just an educational tool. It is also a heartfelt celebration of family, faith, and the power of storytelling. It encourages children to embrace the teachings of the Bible and develop a strong foundation in their Christian beliefs. I hope that as you read this book with your children or share it with your Sunday school class, you will create cherished memories that will last a lifetime. Together, let us instill biblical values in children, nurturing their spiritual growth and guiding them towards a deeper understanding of their Christian faith. Thank you for choosing "Grandma Margie's ABC's of the Bible." May it bring joy, enlightenment, and a sense of wonder to all who embark on this unforgettable adventure. Warmest regards, Dr. K.T. Zulkowski

www.ingramcontent.com/pod-product-compliance
Lightning Source LLC
Chambersburg PA
CBHW041552120626
46551CB00002B/180

* 9 7 8 1 9 6 2 1 0 6 1 6 0 *